THE LITTLE

HIPTIONARY

The Slanguage Dictionary that
Tells It to You Straight Up

RUTH CULLEN

ILLUSTRATED BY

KERREN BARBAS STECKLER

PETER PAUPER PRESS, INC.
WHITE PLAINS, NEW YORK

For Jay, Caroline, and Bryce

Special thanks to
Ian Thrasher for the kewl additions

Designed by Heather Zschock
Illustrations copyright © 2007 Kerren Barbas Steckler

Visit us at www.peterpauper.com

THE LITTLE

HIPTIONARY

Contents

INTRODUCTION

hip·tio·nary *n* (hip + dictionary) **1:** a slan-guage glossary for people in the know; a treasure trove of cool, creative, nonsensical, and playfully irreverent words and expressions for every occasion   *Thanks to* Hiptionary, *I learned how to embarrass my family, shock the neighbors, and impress my friends all at the same time!*

Straight up, this ain't yo momma's English.

But of course not. Language morphs at a *ridonculous* rate. In the time it takes to order a tall, decaf, skinny, whipless, mocha frappuccino with a shot of hazelnut, *phat* has become *crisp! Bad* is so *good* it's *sick! Cool* is not only *kewl*, it's *bangin'*, *tight*, and *sweet*!

How does one keep up? How does one know a *blog* from a *bleg* or a *vlog* from a

 *splog*? Aren't *muffintops*, *cake*, and *cookies* things we eat? Who are *the girls* and why do they need support?

Chillax. Hiptionary's got you covered.

You'll learn some of the hippest new slang, with more than 300 definitions and usage examples arranged alphabetically in chapters organized by theme. You'll find popular idioms and phrases, annoying corporate jargon, and countless ways to say "cool." (How cool is that?)

With *Hiptionary* tucked in your back pocket, you'll have ready access to text talk acronyms and abbreviations (*OMG!*), trendy new terms, classic words from back in the day, and dozens of ways to win at whatever game you play.

You'll even pick up some choice examples of how to sling a few famous—and infamous—names in slang.

If you're looking to interpret your favorite rap lyrics, or you need a primer in teen-speak or techno-talk, you've come to the right place. In no time at all, you'll know the difference between a *wanksta* and a *gangsta*, a *cewebrity* and a *celebutard*—and so much more.

And that's the *truthiness*.

Slang on!

popular slang

All slang is metaphor,
and all metaphor is poetry.

—GILBERT K. CHESTERTON

It rings through high school hallways, billows out of coffee houses, and reverberates off television, computer, and movie screens day and night. We hear it in restaurants, college dormitories, and while standing in line at the bank.

We simply can't escape its reach as we go about the business of our daily lives.

Slang is as old as language itself, helping people of similar backgrounds, interests, and professions identify and connect with one another with a language all their own. At times creatively fun or shockingly crude, the very nature of slang is dependent on who says what and in what context. This can get confusing, as your *bad* might be his *good* and her *cool*.

Popular slang includes idiomatic expressions and everyday words and phrases that have assumed new meanings over the course of time. While much of this new vocabulary may come and go, its very existence is proof that our language is alive and thriving.

Slang is a poor man's poetry.

—*John Moore*

all a·bout *adv* **1:** liking, appreciating, or having enthusiasm for someone or something *I'm all about chocolate.* **2:** emphatic description of one's personal values or beliefs *I'm all about helping the less fortunate, just not my close relatives.*

ass·hat *n* **1:** a foolish or ignorant person *Some asshat in the buffet line keeps eating baby corn like corn on the cob.* **2:** someone whose head is so firmly implanted in his ass that he could wear it as a hat *The asshat driving the yellow Hummer just double-parked in a handicapped spot.*

au·di/au·di 5000 (pronounced "ow-dee") *v:* to leave or depart, used in similar fashion to "I'm outta here" *This party's lame. We're audi.*

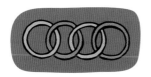

bad·ass *adj* **1:** ultra cool; extremely awesome; also used in the shortened form "bad" *Those are some badass tats you've got on your ankle, Mimi.* **2:** very tough *You seriously don't want to mess with a badass like Coach Johnson.*

bang·in' *adj* **1:** really good; exceptional *That concert was bangin'!* **2:** cool *My iPod rocks the most bangin' tunes.*

beer jack·et *n:* the feeling of warmth one gets after consuming several alcoholic beverages *Without my beer jacket at this football game, the bleachers would feel mighty cold.*

bet·ty *n:* a generic term for an attractive female *There sure are some hot bettys at this party.*

bi·atch/be·yotch/b (pronounced "bee-yotch") —*n* **1:** a kinder, gentler alternative to the derogatory term "bitch"—a malicious, unpleasant, selfish woman—though the term now applies to either men or women *Did that biatch just steal my parking spot?* **2:** a mild and often joking term of disrespect; a diss *Congratulations, biatch. You owned me in bowling.* **3:** a term of quasi-endearment amongst female friends *Do you biatches want to catch a movie later?*

—*v:* to complain or whine; variations include "beotch," "beyatch," "bizatch," "biznatch," and "b" *Kindly shut your pie hole and quit biatching, OK Priscilla?*

bo·gos·i·ty *n:* the degree to which something is bogus or untrue; the state of being false or not genuine *After the accused thief recounted how the jewelry accidentally fell into his shoes, socks, shirt, and underwear, the store detective smiled and said, "I haven't heard that level of bogosity in years."*

bounce *v:* to leave or go *I'm late for class. Gotta bounce!*

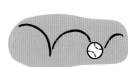

brah/bro *n:* brother; used in the same manner as "homie," "dawg," "dude" and "g" *Sup, brah?*

brand slut *n:* typically, a consumer age 35 or younger who displays no loyalty to any one brand *Judging by all the different designer labels in Carmen's closet, she's a total brand slut.*

broke·back *adj:* of questionable masculinity; giving the appearance of being gay *I don't know, honey. A man day at the spa sounds kinda brokeback to me.*

bug·gin' *v:* acting in a strange manner; freaking out *Leave Bob alone. He's buggin' because he just crashed his girlfriend's car.*
—*adj:* weird or strange *The lady with 50 cats in her one-bedroom apartment is totally buggin'.*

but·ter·face *n:* a female who has an appealing body but an unattractive face; a female about whom everything looks good but her face

Sure, I'd go out with Janice even though she's a butterface.

car·bon neu·tral *adj:* having an environment-friendly quality in which one's climate-damaging carbon emissions are balanced by "green" technologies, such as investing in wind or solar power or planting trees *Sheryll has convinced our entire book club to go carbon neutral next year.*

chill —*v* **1:** to relax or calm down; similar to "chillax" *Chill, Henry. It's just spilled milk!* **2:** to hang out *Let's chill to some John Legend.*
—*adj* **1:** cool; used in the same manner as "tight" and "dope" *Those spinning rims on your Honda look totally chill.* **2:** laid back or relaxed *My roommates are totally chill about my pet snake.*

crisp *adj:* cool or awesome; used in the same manner as "tight," "phat," and "dope" *Those shades are crisp!*

dan·druff *n:* an unreliable, fickle person; a flake *Mary is dandruff. She flakes out on us all the time, saying she'll be somewhere but never showing up.*

dawg/dog/dogg *n:* a close friend; used in the same manner as "bro," "homie," "dude," "man," and "g" *You're barking up the wrong tree, dawg.*

de·li·cious *adj:* a new use of a word that typically applies to food or beverages, meaning pleasing or delightful *Did you see that jump shot? Delicious!*

dope *adj:* cool or awesome; used in the same manner as "tight" or "chill" *The third track on that CD is totally dope.*

down low/dl *adv* **1:** on the sly; secretive or under cover *I got a new job and plan to quit on Friday, but keep that on the down low.* **2:** referring to secret homosexual activities or tendencies of seemingly heterosexual men *Unbeknownst to his wife and children, the governor was leading a dual life on the down low.*

down with *adj* **1:** amenable to something; being accepting or approving of some-  thing *Pizza and wings? Yeah, man. I'm down with that.* **2:** knowledgeable; aware *Oh yeah, teach. I'm down with the periodic table and all the elements.*

drunk dial *v:* to make late-night, regrettable drunken phone calls to an ex girl/ boyfriend or potential romantic interest *Please tell me I didn't drunk dial Sheila at 3 A.M. and* *beg her in baby talk to pwease take me back because I still wuv her?*

e·mo —*adj* **1:** short for "emotional," describing a soft-core punk music genre *Every time you play this emo music, The Ramones start to cry.* **2:** ultra-sensitive, broody, and attention-seeking *Claudia tried to fit in with the emo clique by skulking around school brandishing a journal filled with poems about her horrific upper-middle-class suburban life.*

—*n:* a person immersed in the fashion style characterized by long bangs, tight pants, black-rimmed glasses, and band T-shirts *In the high school cafeteria, the jocks sat with the plastics while the emos clustered in a corner, lamenting their miserable lunches and love lives.*

fo sho/fo shiz·zle *adv:* for sure; really *A sleepover party? We'll be there fo sho.*

four·bucks *n:* slang name for the retail coffee giant Starbucks

Let's plan to meet up at fourbucks this afternoon, mmmkay?

freak *v:* to dance in an obscene manner, complete with pelvic thrusting and provocative grinding  *Debbie, while you've been freaking with Tom on the dance floor, your parents have been watching in horror.*

frick·in' *adj:* a kinder, gentler alternative to the term "f*cking"; used as an intensifier *Who's the frickin' genius who put marshmallows in the toaster?*

friend with ben·e·fits *n:* a friend with whom one occasionally hooks up *I like a job with benefits, so what's so wrong about a friend with benefits?*

ghet·to *—n:* an oft-neglected and crime-ridden area of a city relegated to the poor and disadvantaged; also known as "the hood"

Two wrong turns off the interstate landed Gramps in the heart of the ghetto.

—*adj* **1:** relating to urban life in the poor inner city *Macaroni and chopped-up hot dogs? Um, I love me some ghetto casserole.* **2:** low quality or sub-standard; makeshift; cheap *Dad, the duct tape on your car headlight is so ghetto.*

ghost *v:* to leave or depart, used in similar fashion to "I'm outta here" *Is there a sub today? Cool. I'm ghost.*

Goth—*n:* a Gothic-inspired subculture or person typically characterized by black attire and makeup, and an affinity for hardcore punk or heavy metal music *"Oh my goodness!," the woman exclaimed upon seeing the Goths. "Is it Halloween already?"*

—*adj:* eccentric, dark, mysterious, and weird *Bill experimented with hair dye and makeup* to create a Goth look, hoping he might score some points with the ladies.

harsh my mel·low *v:* to dampen one's relaxed spirit; to ruin someone's mood *Tori watched the news for five minutes and it seriously harshed her mellow.*

hip·a·ti·tis *n:* a disease of terminal coolness *Yo dude, the doctor said I have hipatitis because I'm so incredibly kewl.*

hook up *v* **1:** to meet up with someone; to get together *Let's plan to hook up tomorrow at the mall, OK?* **2:** to have sexual relations with someone, though not necessarily sexual intercourse *Who did you hook up with last night?*

hook-up *n* **1:** a favor, connection, or service *My uncle came through with the hook-up to the concert!* **2:** a person with whom one has had sexual relations

Uh oh. I think I see my hook-up from last weekend standing by the door.

hot·tie *n:* a very attractive or sexually appealing person *Ted cringed when his grandmother introduced him to her friends as, "my grandson, the hottie."*

hum·mer house *n:* a large, pretentious, shoddily-constructed home on a too-small lot clustered together with similar cookie-cutter monstrosities in "upscale" suburban neighborhoods; also known as a "starter castle," "McMansion," or "faux chateau" *The Dinks purchased a hummer house on Nottingham Drive in the Buckingham Hills development near the mall.*

ish *adj:* sort of *Did I like the gift? Yes . . . ish.*

is·sues *n:* a euphemism for problems *Within one month, Jack lost his wife, his job, his house, and one of his kidneys. You could say that he's got "issues."*

it's all good *interj:* an inappropriately positive response to bad news or treatment *"Sorry to keep you waiting for six hours out here in the cold." "Oh, that's OK. It's all good."*

kewl (pronounced "kyool") *adj:* deliberate misspelling and mispronunciation of the word "cool," with the same meaning *Do you think you're extra kewl because you use the word "kewl"?*

Mc *prefix* **1:** a prefix that connotes poor quality or cheapness *Would you like McFries with that McMansion?* **2:** a prefix to a descriptive word, used to sound like a surname *Tonight I'm going out with McHottie, and tomorrow I'll have lunch with McNaughty.*

mo•fo *n* **1:** a kinder, gentler alternative to the offensive term "mother f*cker," a vulgar and insulting term for one who acts in a wholly inappropriate or unacceptable manner *That mofo just stole my car!* **2:** a complimentary term for a friend or someone with admirable toughness or coolness *Man, you look like one badass mofo on that Harley.* **3:** a point of reference when describing the degree to which something is either good or bad *Phoenix in the summertime is hotter than a mofo.*

mo·jo *n* **1:** confidence or self-assuredness *Nora found her mojo during half-time and scored three goals to tie up the game.* **2:** personal magnetism and sex appeal *When Quentin works his mojo, the ladies swarm to him like ants to a picnic.*

mo·net (pronounced "mo-nay") *n:* a person who looks attractive only from a distance *That guy looked like a total hottie but up close he was such a monet.*

muf·fin top *n:* the roll of abdominal flab that spills over the waistband of tight-fitting, low-rise pants *Those extra-low-rise designer jeans do make your butt look small in comparison to your enormous muffin top.*

my bad *interj* **1:** an acknowledgment of fault or blame, without apology or remorse; an insincere apology *My bad? Is that all you have to say after burning down the house?* **2:** an acknowledgment of fault or responsibility *Did I just step on your toe? My bad.*

oh snap *interj* **1:** an exclamation of shock, disbelief, dismay, or joy, used in the same manner as "oh sh∗t" *Oh snap! He's alive! But how? I don't know if I can handle this. Hallelujah!* **2:** an expression used to punctuate an insult *Yo momma's so fat she got her own zip code. Oh snap!*

own *v:* to beat someone at a game; to domi-nate someone or something   *You totally owned the racetrack in the 1,000 meters.*

phat *adj:* a somewhat dated term meaning cool; used in the same manner as "tight," "crisp," or "dope"; acronym for "Pretty Hot And Tempting and Plenty of Hips and Thighs"   *In the nineties, it was very phat to use the word "phat."*

plas·tic *—adj:* attractive and seemingly per-fect on the outside, but shallow and insincere on the inside; fake   *The plastic people always crack over time, a fact many people discover when they attend their high school reunions.*
—n: an attractive person who lacks intellec-tual depth or sincerity; also known as a Ken or Barbie   *Plastics thrive in the club scene because it's all look, no talk.*

plu·to *v:* to be demoted or downgraded, much like Pluto was downgraded from its designation as a planet *Roger got plutoed at work the same day he received new business cards bearing his title.*

ri·donc·u·lous *adj:* incredibly ridiculous or laughable *The* National Enquirer *stories about the Hollywood celebutards are ridonculous.*

se·ri·ous·ly *adv* **1:** a term now used in place of "yeah" or "uh huh" to express agreement *These are the most delicious dirty martinis in town. I know. Seriously.* **2:** a sarcastic use of the word "seriously," meaning, "you can't be serious" *Does he always dress that way? I mean, seriously.*

shut up *interj* **1:** an expression of incredulity or disbelief meaning "no way" or "you've got to be kidding me" *You won the lottery and* *you're moving to Hawaii? Shut up!* **2:** a phrase that means "be quiet," or "shut your mouth" *Would you all kindly shut up? I'm trying to watch the news.*

sick *adj* **1:** awesome or cool; great *That new skateboard park is sick!* **2:** a lot; a significant amount *I have a sick amount of work to do this weekend.* **3:** disgusting or inappropriate *Must you pull the wings off every fly you catch? That's sick.*

slam·min' *adj:* very good; cool *That is one slammin' outfit, LaToya!*

snark·y *adj:* refers to a style of writing or speech infused with snide remarks that have humorous, not negative, connotations; witty, edgy, and sarcastic *I laughed out loud at her snarky comments about corporate culture, though it was quite clear that many of our colleagues didn't get the joke.*

star·bucks·i·an *n:* the language of Starbucks, the retail coffee behemoth that revolutionized the way the world orders coffee  *Excuse me, barista? I ordered a venti skinny whipless half-caf double chocolate chip crème frappuccino with a shot of vanilla, but may I have a tall caramel espresso macchiato instead? Grazie.*

sup/whass·up/what up *interj:* a greeting derived from the expression "what's up" *"Sup, dude?" "Not much. Sup with you?"*

sweet *adj:* awesome or cool; great *Those are some sweet boots.*

tap *v:* to have sex *Did that guy just say "I'd tap that" when we walked by? Ew!*

tat *n:* short for "tattoo" *Lenny, you might consider covering up the tats on your neck, wrists, and ankles when you interview for that job at the bank.*

the girls *n:* affectionate nickname for a woman's breasts *I like this backless dress, but I'll need to do something about the girls.*

tight *adj:* awesome or cool; great; used in the same manner as "sweet," "dope," and "crisp" *Custom wheels and heated seats? This is a tight ride, J-man.*

trip·pin' *v* **1:** acting crazy or strange, as if on drugs; hallucinating *You're trippin' if you think I'm gonna eat Rocky Mountain oysters!* **2:** overreacting *My parents were trippin' when I came home 30 minutes late.*

truth·i·ness *n:* a term coined by Stephen Colbert referring to the quality by which people claim to know something without regard to facts or logic; the truth one wishes to believe; knowledge based on gut feel and instinct that is purported as truth *Truthiness is a word that will not be held back by facts.*

That said, the truthiness of the matter is whatever I want it to be.

uh, hel•lo *interj:* a phrase used to illustrate the obvious, similar to "duh" *So the three-year-old threw a temper tantrum? Uh, hello! Three-year-olds do that.*

va•nil•la *adj:* ordinary; plain *Oh yeah? Do people who lead boring, vanilla lives wear red patent leather stilettos like these?*

wack/whack *adj* **1:** strange or odd; weird *That guy who wants to jump the Grand Canyon with a rocket-powered Vespa is totally wack.* **2:** not cool; bad; unacceptable *I love my Josh Groban CD, even if you think it's wack.*

ward•rob•ing *n:* the practice of returning clothing to a store for a refund after it has been used; also known as "closeting" *The retailers met before the holiday shopping season to discuss how they would deal with the growing problem of wardrobing.*

what•ev•er/what•ev•a/what•ev *interj* **1:** term used when one wishes to dismiss someone or end a conversation *So I forgot to feed your fish and they all died. Whatever.* **2:** a term used to express apathy or frustration *You don't care why I'm leaving you? Whatever.*

what the *interj:* an expression of shock, dismay, or confusion, similar to "what the heck" *No one answered the door so you walked inside, ate their porridge, and fell asleep in their beds? What the?*

whore *n* **1:** someone who acts upon multiple affections for different people, things, or activities *I'm such a whore for cheesecake.* **2:** a woman who uses her body for material gain; a ho *Why do so many talented female singers perpetuate the image of women as whores?*

wife•beat•er *n* **1:** a form-fitting, ribbed, white sleeveless undershirt worn as an outer layer instead of under another shirt; also known as a "tank top," "muscle shirt," or "A-shirt" *Wifebeaters do not suit middle-aged, flabby men with excessive chest hair.* **2:** European slang for Stella Artois beer *Brilliant! Another round of wifebeaters for the lot, indeed!*

Slang *n* the speech of one who utters with his tongue what he thinks with his ear….

—*Ambrose Bierce*

SLANGIN' NAMES

LORENA BOBBITT
Vivian dreamed that she bobbittized her husband in a fit of anger.

GEORGE W. BUSH (DUBYA)
Dubya-speak is a disturbing yet highly entertaining variation of the English language.

ANN COULTER
Has Deborah been possessed by the devil or is she simply acting more Ann Coulterish than usual?

DAVID HASSELHOFF
Don't Hassel the Hoff, babe.

PARIS HILTON
Stay away from that girl. She's a total Paris-ite.

DR. KEVORKIAN
My poor, old, ailing canary seriously needs to be Kevorked.

MONICA LEWINSKY

How dare you try to Lewinsky your way up the corporate ladder!

O. J. SIMPSON

Rumor has it that guy OJ'd his wife!

BRITNEY SPEARS

Her skirt is so short you can practically see her Britney.

MARTHA STEWART

I have to Martha Stewartize the house before my company arrives.

DONALD TRUMP

That comb-over looks Trumpesque, Frank. Lose it.

OPRAH WINFREY

One nation, under Oprah, with liberty and justice for all.

neo slang

By such innovations are languages enriched, when the words are adopted by the multitude, and naturalized by custom.

—Miguel de Cervantes

Some of today's most inventive neologisms, or new words, have been formed by combining two existing words. These blends, also called "portmanteaux," include the prefix of one word and the suffix of another. The resulting term incorporates the definitions of both original words, often in clever or amusing ways.

Thanks to new technologies that allow us to communicate at the touch of a button, neo slang is flourishing.

The more we talk and text our conversations, the more we seek to distinguish and express ourselves with unique and creative vocabulary. When we do, it's only a matter of seconds before an interesting new coinage makes its way around the world.

a·dork·a·ble *adj:* (adorable + dork) adorably dorky *Melvyn was irresistibly adorkable in his argyle sweater vest and plaid pants.*

an·ti·ci·point·ment *n:* (anticipation + disappointment) excitement that quickly fades *Overwhelmed with anticipointment after opening the tiny blue box, she mustered a smile and flung the rare coin out the window.*

bland·wich *n:* (bland + sandwich) a bland, tasteless sandwich *Is it just me or do these blandwiches taste like cardboard?*

bo·gon (pronounced "bow-gon") *n:* (bogus + moron) an ignorant idiot *Did that bogon just say "nu-cu-lar"?*

bo·zone (pronounced "bow-zone") *n:* (bozo + ozone) the impenetrable layer surrounding stupid people that prevents intelligent ideas from getting in *The alarming news about global warming didn't faze the politicians, clearly proving that there were no holes in the bozone layer.*

bride·zil·la *n:* (bride + Godzilla) a woman who becomes increasingly irrational, emotional, unpleasant, and perfectionist as her

wedding day approaches *In the span of six short months, Kaitlin morphed from a sweet, kind bride-to-be into a ferocious, snarling bridezilla.*

Ca·li·forn·i·ca·tion *n:* (California + fornication) the spread of Western popular culture and specifically the commercialization of sex across the world,

epitomized by images from Hollywood, California *Sadly, Californication has led many foreigners to believe that Americans are shallow, amoral, and promiscuous.*

ce·leb·u·tard *n:* (celebrity + retard) a famous person known for displays of stupidity *The celebutards smiled for the cameras as they offered their hand-me-down Prada evening gowns to the starving orphans.*

chill·ax *v* (chill + relax) **1:** to calm down *Forget about your crazy day and chillax, dude.* **2:** to hang out *We're just chillaxin' at my crib.*

crap·puc·ci·no *n:* (cappucci-no + crap) an overpriced gourmet coffee drink that tastes bad *Did I just spend five bucks on this crappuccino?*

crap·tas·tic *adj:* (crap + fantastic) incredibly bad; so extraordinarily bad it's comical *How do I feel after breaking my leg and getting the* *chicken pox? I think "craptastic" pretty much sums it up.*

def·i·not·ly *adv:* (definitely + not) most definitely not *Join you at the monster truck rally this Saturday night? Definotly!*

dread·mill *n:* (dread + tread-mill) the dreaded monotony of walking or running on a treadmill *Martha rewarded* *herself for enduring thirty minutes on the dreadmill with two honey-glazed donuts and a large chocolate frappe.*

fan·tab·u·lous *adj:* (fantastic + fabulous) incredibly good *Yay! I just heard the fantabulous news about your promotion!*

flab·do·men *n:* (flab + abdomen) a flabby midsection *"I simply can't lose weight—especially in my flabdomen," she bemoaned, as she sipped cabernet and stacked cheese cubes on her plate.*

flex·i·tar·i·an *n:* (flexible + vegetarian) a vegetarian who only occasionally eats meat *Belinda tells people she's a flexitarian, but every day at lunch she eats a two-inch thick ham and bologna sandwich.*

fren·e·my *n:* (friend + enemy) a friend who acts more like an enemy *I would classify Fran as a frenemy, because with friends like her, who needs enemies?*

f∗ck·wit *n:* (f∗cking + dimwit) a contemptible idiot *The f∗ckwit not only backed into my car, but he had the audacity to blow me a kiss as he drove away!*

fug·ly *adj:* (f∗cking + ugly) very unattractive *Do you think maybe that couch was reduced for clearance because it's so darn fugly?*

gay·dar *n:* (gay + radar) the innate ability to detect homosexuality in others *He certainly is a hottie, Theresa, but my gaydar frequencies are going haywire.*

ge•ner•i•ca *n:* (generic + America) the same ubiquitous strip malls and subdivisions that have come to define America *Barbara felt right at home as she drove cross country, comforted by the Wal-Mart, Starbucks, Chili's, and Home Depot generica at every turn.*

gi•nor•mous (pronounced "ji-norm-us") *adj:* (gigantic + enormous) extremely large *And there, on the end of my line, was the most ginormous fish I'd ever seen! But then he got away.*

has•bi•an *n:* (has been + lesbian) a former lesbian who now engages in heterosexual relationships *That actress who once dated a very famous female comedienne but is now married with kids is a hasbian.*

ig·no·ra·nus (pronounced "ig-no-ray-nuss") *n:* (ignoramus + anus) someone who is both foolish and contemptible, similar to "asshat" or "f*ckwit" *The ignoranus in charge of the pesticide company told his workers to dump chemical waste into the nearby stream.*

ir·ri·tain·ment *n:* (irritate + entertainment) the annoying and degrading reality-based entertainment and media spectacles one finds impossible to resist *I know he's "the bachelor" and related to that guy you went to college with, but how can you watch this irritainment?*

man·ca·tion *n:* (man + vacation) a men's-only vacation; typically a weekend jaunt during which men bond and relax during rounds of golf, steak dinners, and plenty of beer *Hey guys, for our next mancation, what do you think about deep sea fishing, gambling, and spa treatments?*

man·ny *n:* (man + nanny) a male nanny *The harried housewife giggled like a schoolgirl when she first laid eyes upon her new Swedish manny.*

met·ro·sex·u·al —*n:* (metropolitan + heterosexual) a straight man with an affinity for style, art, culture, and expensive hair and skin care products *At the sight of Bob's man-purse and newly highlighted hair, Sandra simply gave up, declaring, "I'm done, Bob. I just can't date a metrosexual."*

—*adj:* effeminate; stylish, and chic in a typically feminine way *Miriam enjoyed spending time with Claus, despite his metrosexual tendencies.*

mom·bot *n:* (mom + robot) a mother who seems so perfect she must be fake; a well-coiffed, made-up woman wearing stylish clothing or

workout gear who lacks any visible evidence of motherhood *Beth eyed the mombots at the school fundraiser with fear and apprehension.*

pos•i•lute•ly (pronounced "poz-ih-loot-ly") *adv:* (positive + absolutely) most definitely; also known as "absotively" *Will I attend your bowling party? Posilutely!*

pown (pronounced "pone") *v:* (pawn + own) to dominate or own someone so thoroughly you could pawn them off; also known as "pwn" *Tristan, I powned you in* Pictionary.

res•o•lu•tion•ar•y *n:* (resolution + revolutionary) a person who makes a New Year's resolution to join a gym and then quits after a few months *Their good intentions aside, the resolutionaries who swarm the health club in January (aka Joinuary) always disappear by March.*

ring·xi·e·ty *n:* (ring + anxi-
ety) the panic and fear
induced by one ringing cell
phone in a crowd, causing
everyone to scramble for their
phones lest they miss a call *If*
*you suffer from ringxiety every time someone's
cell phone rings, take comfort in the knowledge that you're not alone.*

sac·ri·li·cious *adj:* (sacrilegious + delicious)
pertains to something that is both profane
or in violation of something held sacred,
and pleasing at the same time *The vegetarian savored every sacrilicious bite of filet
mignon and chicken cordon bleu.*

slack•a•dem•ic *n:* (slacker + academic) a perpetual college student; someone who pursues an undergraduate degree full-time for upwards of five years *Seriously, Arnold, you're becoming quite the slackademic. Perhaps if you actually attended class and declared a major, you might graduate sometime this decade.*

tex•tu•al ha•rass•ment *n:* (text + sexual harassment) propositioning or unwanted sexual advances via e-mail or text messaging *For the fourth time today, Dexter, please cease and desist this textual harassment. I do not wish to have dinner with you after work.*

trus•ta•far•i•an *n:* (trust fund + Rastafarian) an overeducated white trust fund baby who lives a hippie lifestyle and talks passionately about third world woes, usually while summering on Nantucket *Although Theodore looks like he was born* *and bred in Woodstock, he's actually a sushi-loving trustafarian with his own private jet.*

u·ber·sex·u·al —*n:* (uber + sexual) the "best" type of man; quintessentially manly yet also stylish, sensitive, and culturally aware *Annabelle hoped that one day an ubersexual brain surgeon would ride up on horseback and carry her off into the sunset.*

—*adj:* manly yet sensitive and refined *Joslyn let out an audible sigh when the ubersexual new employee joined her in the elevator.*

vol·un·tour·ism *n:* (volunteer + tourism) travel that includes short-term volunteer programs *Opportunities for voluntourism in remote corners of the globe have increased exponentially in the last decade.*

wik·i·al·i·ty *n:* (Wikipedia + reality) the truth as defined by consensus, not fact; a term popularized by Stephen Colbert to parody Wikipedia, an online encyclopedia/dictionary in which entries are edited by site visitors and accepted as truth if enough people agree with them *Wikiality is reality as established by the collective conscience, wouldn't you agree?*

win•eaux (pronounced "why-no") *n:* (wine + eau [water]) a playful term used in print to describe wine enthusiasts or connoisseurs who may consume large amounts of wine; a homonym for winos, alcoholic bums who might drink cheap wine or alcohol from a bottle concealed inside a paper bag *The party invitation read, "Calling all Artistes and Wineaux."*

TOO COOL FOR COOL

All that

Awesome

Badass

Bangin'

Boss

Coo

Crisp

Da bomb

Def

Dope

Far Out

Fly

Fresh

Gnarly

Groovy

Hot

Keen

Kewl

Killer

Mad

Mint

Neat

Nifty

Phat

Pimp

Rad

Radical

Sick

Solid

Sweet

Tight

Tubular

Wicked

urban slang

You gotta be born with it, baby.
We walk with the lip, we talk
with the slang. And we pretty.
We pretty, baby. We move like Ali
in his young days. We good with
the jab, good with the stab.

—WYCLEF JEAN

I f you've tried to decipher your favorite rap or hip-hop song lately and come up short, join the crowd.

Urban slang—a catchall for hip-hop slang and word on the street—changes at lightning speed. As soon as fast-talking rap artists bend language to suit their rhymes, an array of new media stands poised to share it with the world.

Unfortunately, by the time these hip new words and patterns of speech trickle down to the suburbs, they're history. Yesterday's news. Out. Straight up.

That said, you might find this lingo enlightening and even helpful—especially if you live in suburbia.

a'ight *interj:* (pronounced "ite") all right *I'll be there later, a'ight.*

all that *adj:* of exceptional quality or degree; superior *Richard think he all that but he just a poser.*

ball·in' —*v* **1:** doing well; being noticeably rich or appearing to live the good life *Check out the Lexus and the bling. Marcus, you ballin'!* **2:** having sex *You ain't ballin' no one, foo, so stop frontin'.* **3:** playing basketball *Yo dawg, I'm a school you later when we ballin'.*

bis·cuit *n:* a hand gun or pistol; revolver *Gimme that dang biscuit so I can busta cap in yo ass.*

biz·ness *n:* matters of personal concern, such as business affairs or sexual activity *My bizness is my bizness, know what I'm sayin'?*

bling bling *n:* **1:** flashy and expensive jewelry often worn by rappers, such as bejeweled medallions or customized grills, oversized diamond stud earrings, and ostentatious rings *Diddy loves to flaunt his bling bling.* **2:** mate-

rial displays of wealth, including luxury cars, planes, yachts, homes, jewelry, and attire *When I become a famous rapper I'm gonna have hella bling bling, yo.*

bling•in' *v:* giving the appearance of wealth, with sparkling jewels, expensive attire, and seemingly the lifestyle to go with them *You blingin' with that iced-out grill, girl.*

boo•ty/boo•tay *n:* a large, curvaceous female posterior; firm, rounded buttocks; also known as "ass," "junk in the trunk," and "badonkadonk" *You might want to check out the rear view of your booty in those jeans.*

boo•ty•li•cious *adj:* attractive and desirable, particularly due to the size and shape of one's buttocks; curvaceous and physically appealing *Bootylicious Beyoncé and her music put the term "bootylicious" on the map.*

bust a cap *v:* to shoot a gun with intent to kill; to discharge a firearm at someone at close range *Chill, g. You don't wanna bust a cap in that punkass wanksta.*

cra•zy *adj* **1:** very good; cool; off the hook *That party was crazy for real!* **2:** mentally deranged *You crazy if you think I'm gonna get up on that horse.*

crunk —*adj:* (crazy + drunk) wild and out of control *I got mad crunk at Dane's party last night.*

—*n:* a rowdy southern rap music style popularized by Lil Jon *Lil Jon might say, "What? What? Yeah! Crunk ain't dead. OK? Yeah."*

—*v:* past tense of crank, meaning "wound up" or "amped" *The music on the dance floor was all crunk up by the time I arrived at the club.*

dead·ed *v:* rejected, ignored, or abandoned; treated as if one is dead; always used in the past tense *I passed Martin in the hallway and he totally deaded me.*

diss *v:* to show disrespect; to insult *Oh no you di'int just diss my shoes.*

fla·va *n:* from the word flavor, meaning personal taste or style *What's your flava, Veronica? More J. Lo, less Lil' Kim?*

fool/foo *n* **1:** a silly or stupid person *No, fool! You don't eat the fortune inside the fortune cookie!* **2:** a quasi-endearing term for a friend *Do you fools wanna catch a movie later or what?*

for real/fo riz·zle *adv:* really, genuinely, and truly; used in a similar manner to "true dat" *I'm so hungry I could eat a horse for real. Did you say you'd eat a horse? For real?*

front —*n:* a legitimate business that is used for illegal money-laundering activities; a cover *The store Benny's Classic Books was actually a front for the West End city mob.*

—*v:* to put on a façade or pretend to be something you're not, either to keep face or impress others *He ain't no gangsta. He just frontin'.*

g *n:* short for gangsta; friend; used in the same manner as "dawg," "brah," "homie," and "dude"; friend *What up, g?*

gang•sta —*n:* one who projects the image of a gang member, with outward toughness, extremely baggy clothing, and a penchant for obscenity-laced language and lyrics about sex, drugs, and violence; the term "gangsta" refers primarily to members of the poor, inner-city underclass, while "gangster" connotes membership or association with organ-

59

ized crime, such as the Italian or Irish mafias *Me and my gangstas just livin' the thug life!*
—*adj:* stylish and cool, in the manner of a gangsta *Those XXXL pants are gangsta!*

ghet•to fab•u•lous *adj:* stylish in a manner befitting the nouveau riche of the ghetto, with flashy designer clothing and accessories, large, expensive jewelry, and pimped-up rides *Jaquan's looking ghetto fabulous with his gold toof and mink hoodie.*

grill *n* **1:** a person's face or teeth *Brush and floss both day and night to keep your grill sparkling white.* **2:** a retainer-like mouthpiece decorated with jewels and metal that fits over the teeth *Kaiya so off the hook with her diamond and platinum grill.* **3:** personal space *Why you all up in my grill?*
—*v* **1:** to quiz or question someone *When I got home, my father grilled me about where I had been.* **2:** to give an intimidating look; to stare someone down *When Bubba walked by and grilled me, I knew I was in trouble.*

hell•a —*adv:* very; extremely *That movie was hella good.*

— *adj:* in large supply or quantity; many or much *Did you see the rims on that bro's Bentley? He must have hella cheddar.*

ho *n* **1:** a woman who uses her body for material gain; short for "whore" in the traditional sense of the word *Stop dancin' the chicken noodle soup like you a ho.* **2:** anyone with questionable morals *Why you hanging out with that good-for-nothing ho?*

holl·a —*interj* **1:** a greeting used to acknowledge someone's presence, similar to "What's up?" *Holla! Sup, y'all?* **2:** a farewell meaning "goodbye" or "talk to you later" *I'm audi. Holla.*
—*v:* to talk to *You some fine-looking ladies. Mind if I holla atchu for a minute?*

hom·ie/home·boy/home·slice *n:* a close friend from the old neighborhood; used in the same manner as "bro," "dawg," "dude," "man," and "g" *My homies always got my back.*

hoop·tie *n:* an old, beat-up car of low functional value that has been cosmetically enhanced with features like dark tinted windows, flashy rims, and spoilers *The fake fur upholstery looks crisp in this hooptie, but I think your engine's on fire.*

ice —*n:* diamonds or diamond jewelry *She's just a poser dripping with cubic zirconia, not ice.*

—*v:* to murder or kill *You messin' wit gangstas, boy, and sooner or later you gonna get iced.*

keep it real *v:* to be true to oneself or one's race; to be genuine *What are you doing, man? Keep it real!*

kick it *v* **1:** to relax; to hang out *We're just kickin' it at Toby's place, watching the game and eating some pizza.* **2:** to hook up with someone in a sexual manner *Hey girl, you wanna come over and kick it for awhile?*

kicks *n:* shoes *Don't step on the kicks, fool.*

know what I'm say•in'? *interj:* a phrase used to emphasize a preceding statement *In a five-minute interview, the famous actress said "Know what I'm sayin?" about a hundred times.*

mad —*adv:* very; extremely *These earrings are mad expensive, but I gotta have 'em.*

—*adj:* in large supply or quantity; many or much *Despite his actions, my bro has mad smarts.*

man up *v:* to act like a "man"; an expression used to remind a man to be tough, brave, confident, and strong; similar to "step up" or "cowboy up" *That was just thunder, boy. Man up!*

of•fie *n:* a nerd or outcast *The students called their eccentric French teacher an offie, to which she always replied, "Qu'est-ce que c'est que l'offie?"*

off the hook/off the hee•zy *adj:* very good or exceptional; cool or hip; also known as "off the chain" *The Usher concert last night was off the hook!*

oh no you di'int *interj:* a phrase that one uses in response to a bold statement or action, meaning "How dare you?" or "You're going to regret that." *Oh no you di'int just eat the last chalupa!*

piece *n* **1:** a gun *How much bank you drop on dat piece?* **2:** a pipe or device used for smoking marijuana *Don't forget to bring your piece and a bag of chips.* **3:** a graffiti master-piece *I dropped a piece on the corner of Third and Main.*

pimp —*v* **1:** to shamelessly self-promote *The young new artist pimped his album to anyone who would listen.* **2:** to embellish or enhance *I pimped my ride with fine Italian leather and a flat screen TV.*

—*adj:* hip or ultra cool; stylish *Zeke felt very pimp in his full-length fur coat and Gucci sunglasses.*

—*n:* a broker of prostitutes; one who exploits women's sexuality for a profit *Get lost, you no good, misogynistic pimp.*

play·a/play·er *n* **1:** someone who manipulates people and/or situations for personal gain *That playa just managed to get himself a table in the VIP lounge and a free bottle of Cristal. He got game!* **2:** a person, usually male, who engages in multiple simultaneous romantic and/or sexual relationships *Forget him, Channelle. Your baby daddy ain't nothing but a playa.*

po-po *n:* the police; also known as "pigs," "bacon," "laws," "five-O" (from *Hawaii Five-O*), and "fuzz" *The po-po met at the donut shop for their daily dozen of Bavarian crème.*

pos•er *n:* someone who pretends to be something he is not; a phony or fraud *T-Bone may look and sound gangsta, but he's just a poser. His real name is Thomas Bonano and he's a political philosophy major at Yale.*

props *n:* proper respect or admiration *Nah, bro. I got mad props for you. I wouldn't diss yo mamma.*

rep•re•sent/rep *v* **1:** to stand for or serve as an example of *I'm here representin' my peeps in the hood.* **2:** to show respect *Stand up and represent!*

ride dir•ty *v:* to drive a car with illegal drugs or weapons in one's possession *Don't you get caught ridin' dirty.*

shor•ty *n:* a girlfriend or attractive female *I'm gonna go holla at that shorty over there.*

shout out *n:* acknowledgment or recognition *I just wanna give a shout out to my homeboys in Hartford, yo.*

sol•id —*n:* a favor performed on someone's behalf *Hey Maria, will you do me a solid and pass me those cheese puffs?*
—*adj:* cool; excellent *Those kicks are solid.*

straight up *adv* **1:** to the point; directly *She straight up told me that if I don't shape up, she's kicking me to the curb.* **2:** truthfully; used in a similar manner as "for real" *I got a job straight up. No foolin'. I start tomorrow.*

true dat *adv:* truly; indeed; an expression used to indicate agreement with someone; similar to "right on" *That Fifty Cent is one bad mofo. True dat.*

wank•sta *n:* a wannabe gangsta; someone who portrays the image of a gangsta but is not an actual gangsta or thug *These wankstas couldn't hustle a book from the library, y'all.*

whip *n:* a car, usually an expensive, luxury model *Nice whip, man. You ballin'!*

word *interj* **1:** a versatile affirmation that can mean "I agree" or "amen" *This album is off the chain! Word.* **2:** a greeting or farewell *Word up, brother.*

SHOW ME THE MONEY SLANG

Bank

Benjamins

Bread

Cabbage

Cake

Cash

Change

Cheddar

Chips

Clams

Coin

Dead presidents

Dough

Duckets

Flow

Loot

Moola

Paper

Rice

Scratch

Smackers

business slang

*Never express yourself more clearly
than you are able to think.*

—NIELS BOHR

The language of business is a curious combination of bureaucratic jargon, ungrammatical posturing, and locker room lingo.

Ever self-conscious and politically correct, new important-sounding words and expressions pop up like weeds and dot the corporate landscape, nourished by a steady stream of monotone and bluster.

In recent years, the vast organizational changes and globalization of the marketplace have spawned new slang terms that are as clever as they are revealing. Clearly, American workers have found a way to maintain their sense of humor and adapt to changing circumstances—with words, at least.

a•gree•ance *n:* a new incarnation of the word "agreement," meaning "state of agreement" *Are we all in agreeance that the term "agreeance" sounds pretentious and stupid?*

al desk•o *adv:* at the desk; usually refers to  eating while sitting at one's desk *I'd love to join you for lunch today, but I'll be dining al desko. This report can't wait.*

ass•mo•sis *n:* process by which a person seems to absorb success and advancement by brown-nosing the boss  *"The only way to get ahead around here is through ass-mosis," Delilah lamented, "so if you'll excuse me, I've got some coffee to fetch."*

a•vi•an fire drill *n:* corporate America's response to a potential avian flu pandemic, including, but not limited to, mandatory meetings, training sessions, official communications, and materials distribution (e.g., "bird flu kits" with flimsy, ill-fitting goggles and porous beanbag masks) *This*

avian fire drill has people so panicked that they stopped serving chicken in the cafeteria.

back of the en•ve•lope *n:* a quick, condensed summary, often in bullet points *C'mon,*

Jenkins. I don't have all day. Just gimme a back of the envelope on the product strategy.

best prac•tice *n:* a management-conceived notion of the most efficient and effective process, method, or technique for accomplishing a goal *No, Bill. We can't just fix the problem and be done with it. The best practice requires that we write up a proposed solution, solicit feedback from the management team, incorporate their feedback into the plan, re-*

distribute the revised plan, make additional revisions as necessary, conduct a mini-test, assess the outcome of the mini test, solicit management feedback on the mini test, and then operationalize the plan—but only if no additional revisions are necessary, in which case we need to . . .

blame·storm —*v:* to sit around in a group making excuses and assigning blame for corporate blunders or missteps; to brainstorm for excuses and scapegoats *While the sales team blamestormed for hours about the failed bid, the support staff played a leisurely game of poker.*

—*n:* a common corporate activity in which people sit around and discuss why something failed and who is responsible *When the dust settled after the blamestorm, only three people remained seated in the conference room.*

boil the o·cean *v:* to attempt an overly ambitious task or seemingly impossible feat of enormous size and scope *Yeah sure. I'll sell*

15 new accounts by Friday right after I boil the ocean.

broad brush —*v:* to describe something in general, as opposed to specific, terms *When the client arrives, broad brush the marketing plan and get some quick feedback.* —*n:* a general overview *Harold starts to glaze after about two minutes, so just give him a broad brush about the action plan and a ballpark of the cost.*

buzz•word-spe•cia•list *n:* a person who seeks to impress others with a vocabulary littered with corporate jargon and industry buzzwords, though often without any real understanding of the terms *To the amazement of his colleagues, Maynard, the resident buzzword specialist, wowed the government auditors with his description of the company's synergistic paradigm for actionalizing best practice learnings.*

cap·size *v:* to downsize a company with disastrous results; to restructure a company in a way that theoretically turns it upside down and sinks it *Betsy's Old-Fashioned Homemade Fudge Factory capsized shortly after it off-shored production to Polynesia.*

con·sul·to·bab·ble *n:* the often indecipherable language of consultants, rich with technical terms, corporate jargon, and clichés *Would someone kindly translate that last statement? I'm not fluent in consultobabble.*

core com·pe·ten·cy *n:* a fundamental set of skills or knowledge required to perform a job *The core competencies for this position include "ability to answer telephone" and "print e-mail documents." So would you please explain why you're asking me to create mathematical formulas on Excel spreadsheets?*

crack•ber•ry *n:* a Blackberry addict; a person who obsessively uses a Blackberry or other wireless handheld device to make phone calls, e-mail, text message, fax, or Web browse *At the support group meeting, Beverly took that crucial first step and admitted she was a crackberry junkie.*

crop dust *v:* to discreetly pass wind while strolling through an office cube farm, fumigating the inhabitants *Much to the dismay of his colleagues, Thomas crop dusted the cube farm every day after lunch.*

cube farm *n:* an open office configuration with a large collection of partitioned cubicles *Amidst the hum and buzz of life in the cube farm, Gloria wondered aloud, "Is this all there is?"*

de·li·ver·a·ble *n:* work; some tangible proof of work activity, such as a report or product, often used to justify fees or expenses  *After nine months of bi-weekly meetings, the only deliverable produced by the Interdisciplinary Management Task Force for Productivity, Excellence, and Efficiency was an empty worksheet with the heading I.M.T.F.P.E.E.*

face-mail *—n:* an increasingly rare form of communication performed face to face *Sally looked forward to receiving daily face-mail from her boss, if only to marvel at his ability to incorporate football analogies into every sentence.*
—v: to communicate face to face *Charles face-mailed Lydia every day as an excuse to pass along the company gossip.*

fire drill *n:* a seemingly urgent matter or imagined crisis; a leadership-driven exercise or initiative that demands significant time and resources *The latest corporate fire drill required all employees to attend a three-hour Handwashing Hygiene training class during which they received antibacterial soap imprinted with the company logo.*

glaze *v:* to sleep with one's eyes open *Sylvester didn't seem to notice that the majority of his audience started to glaze about five minutes into his presentation.*

gran·u·lar *adj:* detailed, as if examining something through a magnifying lens or microscope; down to the nitty gritty *Before sending the newsletter off to the printer, Delores distributed copies of the eight-page document to* *her department associates and instructed them to get granular with each page.*

im·pact·ful *adj:* misuse of the word "impact," meaning to have an impact or influence on something *Charlie, it was very impactful when you said, "There's no 'I' in team" and "Don't be a hero; a hero's just a sandwich."*

le·ve·rage *v:* overused term meaning to act effectively or to influence people *How can we leverage the news about the company scandal?*

mar·ble cei·ling *n:* similar to a "glass ceiling," the barrier that prevents women from advancing in American politics *Speaker of the House Nancy Pelosi believes she broke through the marble ceiling.*

mouse po·ta·to *n:* a person who spends too much time sitting in front of a computer *Don't even bother* *asking Frances to walk with us this week. She's become a total mouse potato.*

ob·fun *n:* obligatory fun, usually in the form of corporate teambuilding exercises or training sessions   *Hoo boy! This team obstacle course challenge is just about more obfun than I can stand!*

off·shore *v:* to relocate some or all company functions to another country to lower costs, usually at the expense of domestic jobs   *Most customer service and tech support functions have been offshored to places like India and Indonesia, so imagine my shock when I reached a real Texas cowboy!*

or·i·en·tate *v:* misuse of the word "orient," meaning to familiarize with new surroundings   *Mindy, will you please orientate our corporate visitors to the conference room?*

out of the loop *adv:* not informed   *Gee, I guess I missed the memo and am out of the loop* *about the fact that all my job responsibilities have been outsourced to Toledo.*

par·a·digm shift *n:* a change from one approach to another; a shift to a new set of beliefs that serve as a model or standard *Fred talks about a "paradigm shift to leverage proactive initiatives," but frankly, Fred wouldn't know a paradigm shift unless it leveraged his proactive initiative right out the door.*

peel the on·ion *v:* to examine something more closely, as if peeling back the layers of an onion skin *The more I peel the onion on that new*  *guy in accounting, the more he starts to stink.*

prai·rie-dog *v:* to stand up and stick one's head above the partition of an office cubicle, much like a real prairie dog sticks his head out of a hole in the ground *When Candace shrieked after spilling hot coffee in* her lap, about 35 heads prairie-dogged at the same time.

re•pur•pose *v:* to re-use material in another form   *The company repurposed the artist's book illustrations as note cards and a calendar.*

re•vi•sit *v:* to return to at a later time   *My boss suggested that we revisit the topic of my proposed raise at a later date.*

RIF —*n:* reduction in force   *Most of the employees were in agreeance that the CEO showed poor judgment by announcing the RIF and then immediately introducing the new executive staff from Bangalore.*
—*v:* downsize; to lose one's job due to staff layoffs   *Ever the blue-sky optimist, Linda described being riffed as being "rightsized," and then started her own business selling stuffed clowns.*

sea•gull ma•na•ger *n:* a manager who flies in, makes a lot of noise, sh*ts on everything, and leaves *You know my seagull manager*  *of a boss is in town when the squawking and the sh*t start to fly.*

stay the course *v:* to persist in a course of action despite criticism or setbacks *The president denied ever supporting a plan to stay the course regarding the international debacle of epic proportions.*

sy•ner•gy *n:* corporate buzzword for teamwork; combination of forces for increased effect or outcome *Irrespective of our personal, professional, intellectual, philosophical, and religious differences, I believe this team has great synergy and will get the job done.*

tri•or•i•ties *n:* three high-priority initiatives that one is expected to manage simultaneously *Suzy made no secret of her triorities at* *work: shop online, make personal phone calls, and go out for coffee.*

val•ue add *n:* a corporate euphemism for a perceived extra benefit or free bonus of a product or service *And when you purchase the Gold Plan, you receive the value add of a customized tote bag and a pen, not to mention the free 24-hour customer service!*

wom•bat *n:* acronym for waste of money, brains, and time *If you ask me, this Corporate Ethics class is (a) an oxymoron and (b) a total wombat.*

ANNOYING CORPORATE JARGON

If hired, what can you *bring to the party*?

Are we all *on the same page* about copy machine protocol?

We really need to *think outside the box* on Secret Santa initiatives this year.

Can we *put* the RIF discussion *to bed* and *talk to* other, more pressing matters, such as the catering menu?

Interesting proposal, Jeffers. Why don't you *run it up the flagpole* and see if you get a salute?

They call it a *reorg* but clearly they're just *rearranging deck chairs on the Titanic*.

How many ways can we *reinvent the wheel*? Haven't we already *been there done that bought the T-shirt* at least a dozen times?

To be truly *impactful* with this group, you should use a *proactive* approach; otherwise, you're just *herding cats*.

You can't *nail jelly to a wall* or *squeeze blood from a turnip!*

Going forward, we must grab the *low hanging fruit* to monetize our assets.

tech and online slang

*Slang is a language that rolls up its sleeves,
spits on its hands and goes to work.*

—CARL SANDBURG

Technology has revolutionized the way we communicate. Nowadays, with the proliferation of computers and the ever-expanding line of slick new gadgets, we use a brand new vocabulary to define the technology and describe its effects on all aspects of our lives. These new words and countless others have made their way into the language of popular culture just as their predecessors (e.g., microwave, remote control, TV dinner) did before them.

The way we use this new vocabulary is another story entirely.

Technology has made us more accessible than ever before. When we're not chatting on cell phones, we e-mail, IM, and text our conversations twenty-four hours a day, seven days a week. The resulting language—a combination of acronyms, shortened words, and phonetic spellings—may be inelegant and a bane to the existence of English teachers around the globe, but it's also highly efficient.

And in this electronic age, the faster, the better.

band•width *n* **1:** technically, the amount of data a network can transfer in a given amount of time, but now used to mean "time" *I don't have the bandwidth for that project.* **2:** by extension, the mental capacity and speed at which a person can process information *If it took Tiffany two days to figure out the tape dispenser, do you honestly think she has enough bandwidth for a high tech copy machine?*

blar•gon *n* (blog + jargon) **1:** the often incoherent gibberish one finds on many blog sites *Dexter, please cut the blargon and write something I can understand, kapeesh?* **2:** a rapidly expanding online language that includes acronyms, numbers, phonetic abbreviations (e.g., CU, UD), and popular slang *Will u plz 86 the blargon on ur MySpace page?*

bleg *v:* (blog + beg) to solicit donations or support on one's blog for a charity or worthy cause *Every time Edgar blegged about the orphaned orangutans in Ouagadougou, Felicia felt compelled to send him a check.*

blog —*n:* (Web + log) an online personal journal in which users post their private thoughts, photos, and videos for public consumption; aptly defined by Marsha TM as "A personal Web page for vain people who mistakenly think that everybody on the planet gives a rats-ass about their business" *Deb, just put down the mouse and back away from the computer. Your blog is no longer an innocent pastime; it's an obsession!*

—*v:* to write and publish a Web log *I blog exclusively about the crafts I make with wine corks.*

blog·ger *n:* a person who spends way too much time behind a computer screen writing blog posts, reading other blogs, and exchanging comments with other bloggers *The parent bloggers bonded over tales of colicky babies and snoring husbands.*

blo·go·sphere *n:* (blog + atmosphere) the burgeoning online world of blogs *Newbies to the blogosphere often lurk for weeks before leaving a comment.*

cell drone *n* **1:** the constant hum of other people's cell phone conversations, especially in enclosed public places such as airplanes, trains, buses, and waiting rooms *I'm sorry. What was that you said? I can't hear you over the cell drone on this train.* **2:** a person who blathers on and on into a cell phone inside an enclosed public place *The cell drone sitting next to me on the plane yakked all the way from New York to L.A.*

ce·web·ri·ty *n:* (celebrity + Web) a person who becomes famous or well-known because of his or her blog or Web site; also known as a "blogebrity" *Quick—find me an agent! With 200 hits on my blog today and a Google rank of #3, I'm practically a cewebrity!*

chips and sal•sa *n:* terms for computer hardware and software, respectively, used primarily by geeks *So I called tech support, and some geek named Dan tells me he wants to check out my chips and salsa, and I'm all, "Whaaaa? Oh no he di'int!"*

cob•web *n:* a seemingly abandoned Web site that has not been updated in years *If you want the low down on global warming, don't waste your time on that government cobweb.*

com•pu•nic•ate *v:* (communicate + computer) to communicate by e-mail, text, or instant message instead of face to face *Why face-mail when you can compunicate? It's quick, easy, and you never have to leave your desk.*

cook·ies *n:* pieces of identifying data that are exchanged between computer servers  and web browsers for the purpose of authenticating users and tracking other specific information, such as site preferences, log-in credentials, and online shopping purchases *Martha could not access the cookie recipe Web site until she enabled cookies on her computer.*

dooce *v:* to get fired from a job due to the content of one's blog, a la cewebrity Heather Armstrong *Uh, hello! When you blog about nasty office rumors and link video footage of your boss wearing the punch bowl at the company holiday party, you should expect to get dooced.*

drail *v:* to send e-mails while drunk *Damn! When will I learn that martinis and mouse clicks don't mix! Not only did I drail my entire address book last night, but I "won" more than $500 worth of used fishing tackle on eBay.*

dub dub dub *n:* short for "World Wide Web," or "www," the beginning of an Internet address *Does anyone have the dub dub dub for that new office supplies vendor?*

e-zine *n:* an electronic magazine which may feature sound, video, and/or interactive technologies *On my lunch hour I can usually be found at my desk eating fast food and reading health-related e-zines.*

fat fin·ger *v:* to make a spelling error while typing

Are you sure he meant to say "I lick your blof"? He probably just fat fingered "I like your blog."

flame *v:* to send inflammatory or hostile e-mail or text messages

When Flanders learned he didn't get the promotion, he flew into a rage and flamed his boss, his boss's boss, and the entire board of directors.

flam·er *n:* a person who sends obnoxious e-mail or text messages *Flamers are a total pain in the net.*

flog *n:* a fake blog; a blog created solely for the purpose of promoting products or services *The author/budding politician created a flog on which he could sell his book and advance his political agenda.*

geek *n* **1:** a person who is passionately interested in technology, computers, or electronic media, though not one necessarily lacking in social skills;  a hacker *Bill Gates is undeniably the world's most famous geek.* **2:** a person who pursues a unique interest with great passion or intensity; the terms "geek" and "nerd" are not synonymous *The bird-watching geeks met every Sunday morning before dawn hoping to spot a rose-breasted grosbeak.*

geek chic *adj:* fashionable in a unique but oddly appealing style befitting a geek, complete with thick, black-rimmed glasses and a pocket protector *Lester in IT*  *had a geek chic magnetism that Phyllis in Purchasing found impossible to resist.*

geek speak *n:* the technical language of computer geeks; also known as "technobabble" or "computer jargon" *"Knock Knock!" "Who's there?" "JavaScript html RSS UNIX." "JavaScript html RSS UNIX who?" "Gah! I forgot the punch line with all this geek speak."*

goo·gle *v:* to search for information online using Google or another search engine *On quiet Saturday nights, Harold would sit in front of the computer with a big bowl of popcorn and google the names of old girlfriends.*

hack —*n* **1:** a negative term for an incompetent or inefficient computer programmer or networker *What the . . . OK, who let the company hacks mess with my computer again?* **2:** derogatory name for a second-rate writer *After her second glass of chardonnay, Claudia*

shocked her fellow book club members by dismissing the book as "the craptastic reflections of a talentless hack."

—*v* **1:** to employ great artistry, wit, and technical genius in designing computer programs or systems *Louis hacked into the wee hours of the morning and finally succeeded in getting the program to work.* **2:** to break into computers and disable security systems *Ashley hacked into the school computer system and modified her less than stellar attendance record.* **3:** to accomplish a computer programming goal through inelegant or inefficient means; to jury-rig *We hacked this component to meet deadline, but we'll do it correctly now that we have the time.*

hack•er *n* **1:** an expert computer programmer or networking wizard; an enthusiastic and knowledgeable computer user who enjoys the challenge of building networks and solving technical problems *The hackers came to Reverend Johnson's aid after a pornado struck the church computer and disabled the mouse.* **2:** a rogue computer user who applies his or her technical knowledge to break into computers and disable security systems *Some adolescent hacker managed to breach security at the White House by using the screen name "Dubya" and the password "laura4eva."*

hack·ti·vist *n:* (hacker + activist) someone who uses his computer programming and/or technical expertise to promote a political cause, often by destructive or disruptive means; electronic civil disobedience *Anti-fur hactivists launched a cyber-attack on the Web site of the world's largest fur coat manufacturer, temporarily freezing all activity and revising their banner to read, "Love animals. Don't wear them."*

i·plod *v:* to walk around in public oblivious to one's surroundings while listening to music

 from an iPod *As the sweet sounds of Beethoven's Piano Concerto No. 5 echoed in his ears, Chester inadvertently iplodded into the path of an oncoming bus.*

lurk•er *n:* someone who frequents chat rooms and blog sites without ever leaving a comment *Lurkers may lurk but they can't hide, thanks to free, invisible Web tracking technology that identifies site visitors by location, IP address, ISP, and so much more.*

lu•ser *n:* (loser + user) a term for someone lacking basic computer skills or common sense *At any given time, you will find dozens of lusers calling tech support to learn how to plug in their computers.*

My•Space junk•ie *n:* a person with a compulsive need to view MySpace pages, especially their own; also known as a "MySpaceaholic" *Alice has become such a MySpace junkie that she gets up at least three times a night to check for new comments.*

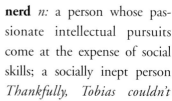

nerd *n:* a person whose passionate intellectual pursuits come at the expense of social skills; a socially inept person *Thankfully, Tobias couldn't hear the children's taunts of "nerd" through his Vulcan ears.*

ne•ti•quette *n:* (Internet + etiquette) rules and guidelines for online politeness established by the Internet community *Trolls who send flaming e-mails IN ALL CAPS need to learn some netiquette.*

ne•ti•zen *n:* (Internet + citizen) an active member of the Internet community *The online community continues to grow and flourish thanks to the good netizens of the world.*

new•bie *n:* a newcomer to the online community; someone who is new to a game, the Internet, a chat room, or various technologies; also known as a "newb" *Would someone please tell that newbie to read the FAQ?*

noob *n:* a derogatory term used primarily by Internet gamers for an obnoxious and/or incompetent person; also n00b *Isn't this the noob who routinely gets killed off in the first five seconds of every game?*

phish *v:* to entice unwitting users to share sensitive personal information such as passwords and credit card numbers by baiting them with fraudulent e-mails and look-alike Web sites for legitimate organizations; to conduct an online scam *Criminals who have a solid command of the English language could phish more successfully than those who don't, since bad grammar and misspelled words tip off the scam every time.*

por·na·do *n:* a virtual tornado of pornographic pop-up windows, often a consequence of viewing online pornography or responding to lures such as "Grand prize win-ner" *Unfortunately, many young children have been swept up in pornados while conducting harmless Internet searches.*

se•ri•al text•er *n:* a person who constantly sends and receives text messages *Much to his parents' dismay, Roger was a serial texter who could not refrain from sending text messages at the dinner table.*

spam *n:* unsolicited mass e-mail, text, or pop-up messages that overwhelm inboxes and network servers; online junk mail *Why is it that most spam e-mail messages advertise products for penis enlargement?*

splog *n:* (spam + blog) a blog containing  nonsensical text or stolen content designed for the sole purpose of linking to and promoting another site; an advertisement disguised as a blog; also known as "blam" *The* *blog name "Loan Refinance Now" should have alerted me to the fact that this was a splog.*

troll *n:* a person who leaves inflammatory or provocative comments on blogs, message boards, and elsewhere to spur an angry or disruptive exchange *If trolls can't say something nice, why must they say anything at all?*

vlog *n:* (video + blog) a video Web log that typically features the personal thoughts and experiences of the creator, usually with supporting text; vlogs may also document news events, politics, business, instructional how to's, and every other topic imaginable *Alan's vlog showcased his many talents, most notably his ability to moon-walk while singing Broadway show tunes.*

wa•rez *n:* pirated computer software, games, movies, music, and other intellectual properties that are widely distributed over the Internet in violation of copyright laws; computer software whose copy-protections have been "cracked" and illegally shared *Unbeknownst to his parents, Wally spent the entire evening downloading warez instead of doing his homework.*

yel·lu·lar *adj:* loud and obnoxious, in the manner of cell phone users who shout into their devices *My mother goes all yellular every time she uses a cellular phone.*

TEXT TALK

2 = to

<3 = a heart or love

4 = for or four

?4u = question for you

4nr = foreigner

86 = out of or over

i <3 u or 143 = I love you

411 = information

404 = I haven't a clue (from the HTTP Error 404 Not Found message)

afk = away from keyboard

b4n/bfn = bye for now

bamf = bad ass mother f*cker

bcuz = because

bff = best friends forever

brb = be right back

btdt = been there done that

btw = by the way

c = see

cu = see you

cya = cover your ass or see ya

cyl/cyl8r/cul8r = see you later

da = the

f2f = face to face

g2g/gtg = got to go

gr8 = great

h8 = hate

hoas = hold on a second

idk = I don't know

imho = in my humble opinion

irl = in real life

iyss = if you say so

jk = just kidding

k = OK

kma = kiss my ass

l8r = later

lmao = laughing my ass off

lol = laughing out loud

meh = neither yes or no

mmmkay = OK

mwah or muah = evil laugh

n00b = obnoxious and/or incompetent person

ne1 = anyone

nuff = enough

omg = oh my god

plos = parents looking over shoulder

plz = please

pwnd = defeated; beaten, as in a game

qt = cutie

rofl = rolling on the floor laughing

sete = smiling ear to ear

sis = snickering in silence

slap = sounds like a plan

stfu = shut the f*ck up

tbd = to be determined

tyvm = thank you very much

u = you

ud = you'd

ur = your or you're

wtf = what the f*ck

wth = what the hell

xlnt = excellent

y = why

sports slang

*I don't know much Japanese, but
we've taught them all kinds of English
slang to help lighten the mood.
Like, "What's up, kid?"
"What's up, dawg?" and
"Come on, dude."*

—PITCHER DAN SERAFINI,
ON HIS JAPANESE TEAMMATES

If you've ever sat in a dugout, huddled on a field, warmed a bench, or spent time in a locker room, athletic arena, sports bar, or country club, you know the bottomless pit that is sports slang.

And if you've ever tuned in to sports radio, or watched sports-related recaps on cable TV or the evening news, then you understand just how vivid, metaphorical, and dramatic the language with which we describe our favorite pastimes can be.

Sports slang, and particularly words and expressions from the game of baseball, is so deeply ingrained in our culture that we may not realize the extent to which it peppers our everyday language. We *step up to the plate*, *pitch ideas*, *drop the ball*, and *play hardball*— all without setting foot on a field.

But whatever the sport, the analogy is a natural one. The battles we wage in sports easily translate to the challenges we face in life. And wherever we are, make no mistake about it, we want to win. Just as the Eskimos may have hundreds of words for snow, we have at least that many to describe exactly how and to what extent we will dominate—and decimate—our opponents.

The following terms and expressions are but a brief sampling from the world of sports.

air·mail *v:* to over-hit a golf ball past the green or an intended target   *Chris slammed his nine-iron into a tree after he airmailed his shot at least 200 feet beyond the green.*

all net *adj:* in basketball, describing a successful shot that doesn't hit the backboard or the rim; also known as a "swish" or "string music"   *Did you see that shot? All net, baby. All net.*

ba·gel *v:* in tennis, to beat someone 6-0   *Julie double-bageled her opponent in 51 minutes without even breaking a sweat.*

bank shot *n:* in basketball or billiards, a shot that bounces off the backboard or cushion before it drops into the basket

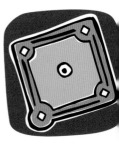

Mike, a geometry teacher, used his understanding of angles to master the bank shot.

boo-yah *interj:* an exclamation used when celebrating a victory or expressing joy; similar to "boomshakalaka" *I do believe I win again. Booyah!*

but•ter•fin•gers *n:* a clumsy person who cannot seem to catch or hold onto a ball *The crowd let out an audible gasp when the butterfingers playing tight end missed an easy pass.*

can of corn *n:* in baseball, an easy-to-catch fly ball *"C'mon, Mayes!" the coach yelled from the dugout. "How could you miss that can of corn?"*

dance floor *n:* the putting green on a golf course *To the detriment of her golf game, Barbara always seemed to get jiggy on the dance floor.*

dirt·ball·er *n:* in tennis, a clay court specialist *Rafael Nadal has proven himself to be an excellent role model, not to mention a world-class dirtballer.*

grape smug·gler *n:* a small, tight-fitting, Lycra swimsuit for men; also known as a "banana hammock" or "mankini" *Frank, Reub, and five other retired men wearing grape smugglers meet at the YMCA pool each morning at six o'clock.*

hat trick *n:* three goals or successes in a row *When Aaron scored three goals in the game, his twin brother Benjamin screamed, "You got a hat trick!"*

head•er *n:* in soccer, a shot in which a player uses his head to hit the ball *Anna jumped high enough to intercept the pass and hit a header into the goal.*

hot dog *n:* a person who shows off or performs dangerous, attention- 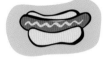 seeking stunts; if young, known as a "cocktail frank" *That hot dog on the skateboard did a triple flip off the curb and nearly crashed into a parked car.*

juice —*n:* steroids *Three months after starting his juice regimen, Tyrone's muscle mass noticeably increased.*
—*v:* to take steroids *The professional baseball player denied juicing and attributed his*

impressive physical appearance to diet and exercise.

kit·ty lit·ter *n:* in golf, a sand trap; also known as "the beach" *Despite his perfect swing, Dan sank his ball deep in the kitty litter.*

Mon·day morn·ing quar·ter·back —*n:* someone who second-guesses or passes judgment on something, such as a Sunday night football game, after it has occurred; a hindsight critic *The Monday morning quarterbacks prattled on and on about the coach's decision to go for it on fourth down.*

—*v:* to second-guess or criticize something after it has occurred *Al Monday morning quarterbacked one time too many, and the players let him know it.*

nut•meg *v:* in soccer, to kick the ball between the defender's legs, run around him, and continue dribbling the ball down the field *Kent was mortified when Michael nutmegged him in the first half.*

or•gan do•nor *n:* person who refuses to wear a helmet while cycling *Some organ donor cruised past me on the downhill going well over 50 miles per hour.*

shred *v:* in skiing or snowboarding, to hit the slopes powerfully and aggressively *Did you see the way Tom and Sara shredded that mogul run?*

take the rock to the hole *v:* take the ball to the basket *As Alex dribbled the ball down the court, his parents yelled, "Take the rock to the hole! Take the rock to the hole!"*

throw up a brick *v:* in basketball, to make a bad shot and miss the basket *Instead of sinking a*

three-point shot to win the game, the Hoopsters
threw up a brick just as the buzzer rang.

worm·burn·er *n:* in baseball or golf, a hit ball
that moves along the ground fast and hard
David slammed a wormburner past the third
baseman and out into left field.

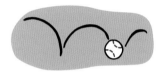

yard sale —*n:* a spectacular fall or wipeout
while skiing or snowboarding in which hats,
goggles, skis/snowboards, poles, and other
equipment get scattered over a large area; also
known as a "starfish" *Jude's cheeks blushed a*
deep crimson as the skiers on the chairlift
above shouted out "Ten!" and applauded her
yard sale.
—*v:* to fall or wipe out and leave a trail of
equipment and belongings *On the last run of*

the day, Cindy flew over a mogul at high speed and yard saled right in front of the ski lodge.

ze•bra *n:* a referee wearing a black and white striped uniform *"Send this zebra back to the zoo!"* the hockey fans jeered.

BEAT YOU?
LET ME COUNT THE WAYS...

Bash	Juice
Beat	Lace
Belt	Laser beam
Blaze	Lash
Blister	Nail
Clip	Own
Clock	Paste
Cork	Pepper
Drill	Plank
Hammer	Pole
House	Pound

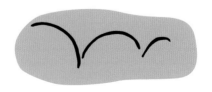

Powder	Slug
Pown	Smack
Pummel	Smash
Ram	Smoke
Rap	Spank
Rip	Sting
Scald	Stroke
School	Whack
Scorch	Whang
Shellack	Whip
Slap	

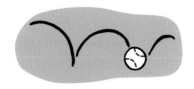

EVERYDAY BASEBALL SLANG

Richard was *caught off base* by the unmarked police cruiser.

Marilyn decided to *cover her bases* by serving a vegetarian entrée with the main course.

Who *dropped the ball* and got us so far behind on the new logo design?

Caroline sent out party invitations in an attempt to *get the ball rolling*.

Let's try to *get to first base* by scheduling a meeting.

Bryce said he would *go to bat* for me if my proposal is challenged.

Madelyn, you really *hit a home run* with those chocolate cupcakes.

Is this price range *in the ballpark*?

Sara struggled to *keep her eye on the ball* despite the many distractions of college life.

How will we ever *level the playing field*?

You have to be really *on the ball* to finish your Christmas shopping in July.

Her idea about sculpting the model out of cheese was *out in left field*.

Diane, will you *pinch hit* for me while I'm in Bermuda?

Let's *pitch* the story idea and see what they say.

Do we want to *play ball* with this company?

The negotiators made it clear they were *playing hardball.*

Right off the bat, Heather bought sunglasses and a short blonde wig.

Martha knew it was time to *step up to the plate* and get the job done.

Andrea gave it a try, even though she feared she might *strike out.*

You win some and you lose some. That's just *the way the ball bounces.*

I'll call you next week to *touch base.*

classic slang

*I've found that there are only two kinds
that are any good: slang that has established
itself in the language, and slang that you
make up yourself. Everything else is apt
to be passé before it gets into print.*

—RAYMOND CHANDLER

History has a knack for repeating itself —which can be both a blessing and a curse.

Cultural remnants from yesteryear can be stylishly classic (think: derby hats and vintage jewelry) or . . . not (think: high-waisted skinny jeans).

In the case of language, many words and phrases once considered hip can certainly relive their heyday depending, of course, on who says them and in what context. "Peace out" is currently back in the mainstream, if in fact it ever left. But what about some of the other playful and unique terms from days gone by? Isn't it time we dusted them off and gave them new life?

Classic slang as it appears here may still be considered hip to some (*Holla grandma!*), and to others, well, it may become very much in fashion when spoken by you.

bee's knees *n:* excellent or wonderful; the best; similar to "cat's pajamas" *Isn't this flapper dress with the beaded fringe the bee's knees?*

cool beans *adj:* cool or great; awesome *You're coming to the party? Cool beans!*

cri•mi•ny *interj:* an exclamation of surprise or frustration; a euphemism for "Christ" similar to "crikey," "cripes," and "Christmas" *Criminy! I just backed the car through the garage door!*

ducks in a row *n:* expression used to mean orderliness, organization, or preparedness

Do you have your wallet, ticket, and suitcase? Great! It looks like you have all your ducks in a row.

e•gads *interj:* an exclamation of surprise or mild frustration; a euphemism for "Oh God"

Egads, mother! How much hot sauce did you add to this chili?

fix his wa·gon *v:* an expression meaning to punish or get even with someone; to get revenge *These automatic sprinklers will really fix his wagon next time he tries to curb his dog on my lawn.*

flib·ber·ti·gib·bet *n:* a flighty, scatterbrained person; a dingbat *Stop being such a flibbertigibbet and make up your mind!*

fly by the seat of one's pants *v:* to do something on the fly without the necessary experience; to improvise *The men never installed electrical wiring before and were flying by the seat of their pants.*

food·ie *n:* a person who is keenly interested in cooking and eating different types of food and cuisine; a gourmet *The foodies jostled for space outside the new restaurant, hoping to* get a table and sample the Ethiopian fusion cuisine.

fox *n:* an attractive and sexually appealing person *Back in the day, Marilyn Monroe was considered a real fox.*

gad•zooks *interj:* an exclamation of surprise or frustration *Gadzooks! There seems to be a streaker on the field!*

groo•vy *adj:* a popular term from the 1960s meaning cool or awesome *This tune is groovy. Can you dig it?*

hea•vens to bet•sy *interj:* an expression of mild shock or surprise *Heavens to Betsy! David just dropped the Thanksgiving turkey on the floor!*

hu•lla•ba•loo *n:* a great noise or commotion; uproar *What's all this hullabaloo about trans fat? Can we talk about it over some bacon cheeseburgers and fries?*

jee•pers cree•pers *interj:* a euphemism for "Jesus Christ," similar to "cheese and crackers" or "Jiminy Christmas" *Jeepers creepers! Don't jump out and scare me like that!*

lol•ly•gag *v:* to relax; to pass time in an idle manner *I wish you folks would quit lollygagging and clean up this mess!*

mack dad•dy *n:* a slick, sharp-dressing man; a pimp *Who's the blingin' mack daddy in the pinstriped suit?*

natch *adv:* naturally *I wore a navy blazer, a white blouse, and my favorite khaki pants, natch.*

nif•ty *adj:* cool or great; used in the same manner as "neat," "keen," "spiffy," or "peachy" *When Chad gave Sylvia a nifty new necklace with spiffy earrings to match, she gushed, "Oh Chad. You're so neat! These are peachy!"*

peace out *interj:* good-bye; see you later *Peace out, dudes! See you next week at the rally!*

rap·scal·lion *n:* a rascal or playfully mischievous person; used in a similar manner to "scalawag" *Come back here this instant with my reading glasses, you rapscallion!*

road piz·za *n:* road kill; animal remains on roads or highways *The animal conservationists swerved to avoid some road pizza on their way to the environmental center.*

ske·dad·dle *v:* to leave quickly; to hurry off *It's getting late so we better skedaddle.*

spend a pen·ny *v:* to go to the bathroom; from the days when public restrooms cost one penny *If you'll please excuse me, I've got to go spend a penny.*

spill the beans *v:* to divulge secret information *Whatever you do, don't spill the beans about the surprise party!*

stud muf•fin *n:* a sexually appealing man *I can't believe a total stud muffin like Trevor even noticed me, let alone asked me to the dance!*

swell *adj:* excellent *I had a swell time on our date, Chas.*

swish *adj* **1:** cool or hip *Doesn't Arnold look swish in that tuxedo?*

2: effeminate *The drag queen's swish mannerisms carried over into his construction job.*

whip·per·snap·per *n:* a bratty youngster *Listen here, young whippersnapper! Keep your ball out of my flower garden!*

who did it and ran *adj:* an expression meaning "looking terrible" and implying that one was beaten up *You'll have to give me a minute or two. Right now I look like who did it and ran.*

yikes *interj:* an exclamation of fear or surprise *Yikes! Is that mullet part of your new look?*

INDEX

A

B